123

What Can You Grow Up to Be?

By Josée Lavoie

*To Mom & Dad, for always
encouraging me to chase my dreams.*

Copyright © 2022 by Josée Lavoie

All rights reserved. The translation or reproduction of any excerpt of this book in any manner whatsoever, either electronically or mechanically and, more specifically, by photocopy and/or microfilm, is forbidden.

123 What Can You Grow Up to Be?
© Text by Josée Lavoie. 2022
© Illustrations by Josée Lavoie. 2022

Published by Josée Lavoie

HeyJosee.com

ISBN:
978-1-7781934-2-2 (Paperback)
978-1-7781934-8-4 (Hardcover)
978-1-7781934-9-1 (eBook)

First Edition, 2022

When you grow up, you can become a dentist, a mail carrier, or even an athlete!

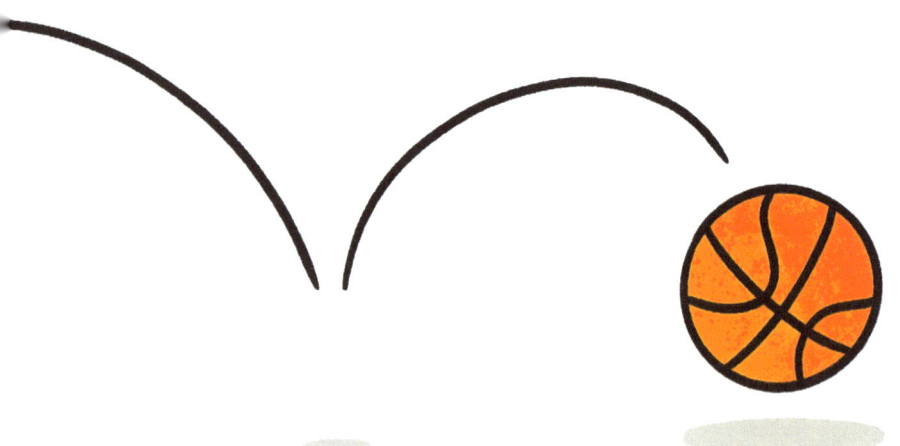

Learn the numbers from **1 to 10** and discover what you could be!

Vivian the ventriloquist makes **one** puppet talk.

Steve the server brings **two** milkshakes.

Marco the magician makes **three** doves appear.

Carol the crocheter made **four** mittens.

Patrick the pastry chef made **five** macarons.

Cameron the construction worker places **six** cones.

Fiona the farmer harvests **seven** carrots.

Xander the xylophonist plays **eight** keys.

Stella the scientist studies **nine** butterflies.

Alice the astronaut spots **ten** stars.

10

Now you know the numbers from 1 to 10

Did you discover what you could be?

www.ingramcontent.com/pod-product-compliance
Lightning Source LLC
Chambersburg PA
CBHW041541040426
42446CB00002B/189